Anti-Nationalist

Anti-Nationalist

A collection of new poems by Byeon Yun-je
Translated by Julie Wi

반국가세력 변윤제

K-Poet Series 045

ASIA

Contents

Part One

Part Two

ANTI-NATIONALIST

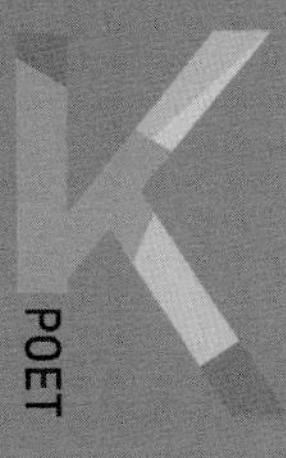

Part One:
Anti-Nationalist

Nostril Dream

This place tells me there are still spaces in me to
be dug into
But it tells me, not too deep
At times, I clump
Or drip down
To form rumors

This coastline is like the tip of your nose
Seaside caverns hold in a dark cough
You are
Within nostrils
Clinging to murmurs, your protective weapon
Rumor
Rumors

Many words surround you and me
You make a shield of your mumbles
Better to be plagued by your own words
Than theirs

From countless self-fabricated rumors
I am dripping
Sometimes clumping
It's all a nostril's dream
Figures march into left nostril
Emerge from right nostril
What difference is there between deceit and discourse?
Between cowardice and compromise?

The seaside village is all talk of nostril dreams

One village borne of divine rhinitis
Nostril
My dear nostril
I write a letter to my holes
Someone who approaches your holes
In a place words cannot reach
Not mine
Not yours
Sniff, and snuff them out
Let unknown flow into unknown
We must make an oath
To clump and harden

What prayers will be answered?
What joys will break free from nostrils
To soar into the gaping sky?
Unknowable things
Unknowable places
A very long time in the village of nostrils

Someday far into the future
All of this will be like a nostril
Just like a booger
At most, I like you
At most, you like me
It's all one big nostril
A nostril dream

All that's left now is to breathe slowly
Colossal winds and
Fresh, crisp air fills your belly to the brim
In the end, your holes
Will help you to breathe

(Anti)Nationalist

Anti-nationalist.
Anti-nation.
Anti.

Apparently, I said those words three times before stirring awake. Eyes breaking open with a shout. Clutching my innocent blanket—poor polyester—to my chest

You anti-nationalists!
You can't even keep the people warm!

What's this then? If you were a fifty thousand won blanket, delivered by a rocket. What

would you think of the white fuzz escaping
your fibers? Rustling to the touch. Forming
clouds when blown away. Falling limply when
thrown

But when ignited:
Engulfing his house—this neighborhood—in
flames.
A tremendous possibility

Does the blanket see its balls of fuzz as
insurgents?
Its white lint's quiet detachment as treason?

The window slides open
A sleepless night
A withering tree leans on the neighbor's stone
  wall. A swarm of flies congregates nearby.
  Buzzing wings. Grand citizens of a nation

Could insect wings run along those logs?
Could dung-fly citizenship
And humming noises
Be issued to each one?

Military vehicles dispatched at dawn
Gun barrels aimed at the Yeoido morning

This night, a bullet of darkness shot from the
muzzle

Reality surpasses imagination
Imagination exceeds reverie

Foolish, useless poet
I snatch reverie's wings and crack the whip

Anti
Anti-nation
Anti-nationalist

I launch words starting with "anti" into the

distance

Antipathy
Anti-gravity
Anticipate
Ablaze

The abdomen of a firefly illuminates when air
rushes in
Insects flying straight to space
A Big Bang of sorts

My imperfect god blew air into fireflies.

Could that be how the universe began?

I will stand, if I must
Against not the country, but the world.
Against not the world, but the universe.

I'll be… I'll be… anti-universalist.

In my wooden boat, guns as oars, I pierce
through ethereal clouds, launch myself
towards the tyrannical andromeda.

Underwhelming,
anti-nationalists.

Towards the galactical empire and dung-fly
espionage.

Now the swarm of dung flies is a black hole
Crackle, thunder
A pitch-black energy wave resounding from the
earth.

Finally, from somewhere
The sound of the World Tree falling

Over the window, I shake my blanket to scatter
the dust. In truth, I am surrendering. My

loss was decided before birth. I'm a good
person—really

I hang up a white blanket instead of a flag
To deceive the universe

This isn't a flag at all, but a blank page

Yes,
It's a snowstorm

If all the world's blankets were shaken,
The dust would kick up a blizzard
Vicious enough to smother everything

Gloomy and ominous,
Pouring down
From the sky—no, space

Massive, microscopic, and yet tremendous white particles

Is that right?
Anti-nationalists.

Flying from fabric

Hypothermia

Every last one freezes to death

I can't even keep the people warm!
Anti-nationalist!
That's the stuff!

Bzz, bzzzzz

I am a flame that sheds light, but never warmth

Sinister Soy Sauce Poem

That asshole, I can't believe it
I can't
That's what you said

Again and again
When you were fired from your workplace
Before the holidays

At a Tonkatsu restaurant in Mangwon
You said that faith could exist
Without religion

You were hunched in the corner of the Japanese
restaurant

I could smell soy sauce from your thin, pursed
lips—yes,
"Faith" came from your mouth reeking of soy
sauce

I hope that savory smell crosses over to heaven

That we'll ascend with the fermented odor of
doenjang and natto,
Not a speck of gold,
Or pearly-white to be seen

You'll flip
The topic of conversation, over and over

From cursing your coworkers, to how soy sauce is the base of all Japanese cuisine, to how you like Jesus for overturning those tables to defend a prostitute and driving away money changers with a whip

A pastor once said
That Heaven could preserve life's subtle flavors.

Now, wait a minute.
Does that mean
There might be temp jobs in heaven?
Unjust termination and
Employment scams?

What if we made angel wings out of spilled soy
sauce
And got chummy while
We talked about death

Over katsu-don
Sake-don and
Udon nabe with kimchi to top it off

Let's take this somewhere else we're already at
our third restaurant, should our fifth be in
heaven or hell maybe we could vent a bit at
the next spot and head to your place

What a silly doctrine
To ignore chili flakes in your teeth
To believe those flakes want to be stuck there

On some island in Africa
They say some monkeys have entered the stone
age, stacking rocks pointlessly, collecting the
bones of their companions. *You don't say.*

Sign of the cross
Made from woolly mammoth's bones
I watch fermented leftovers as
Literature,

Poetry and
Other pointless things abound

In life, there are things we cannot control
Things that can't be believed
Things outside of faith

I guess
We could really call this a life
Or a poem
Sinister-soy-sauce poem

When we parted ways that day
You almost got hit by a motorcycle

Hahaha
Ahahah
You started shouting

Saying the sound wasn't there because of the
motorcycle
The motorcycle was there
Because of its sound

A sinister soy sauce poem

The smell makes it complete

An angel may have comrades
But a devil has friends

We'll be miserable for the rest of our lives
Not you
Not me

Us!
Ahahaha
Hahahah

Stone Pillow Principle

The pillow where the dreamer's head rests
   becomes lighter. Flowing locks. All those
   inauspicious horsehairs.
You see, the dreamer's nightmares gobbled up
   all his bedding

That's why I made myself a stone pillow. I
   wanted to launch pebbles into the air
I was concocting a dream of scattering pebbles.
   Spewing fog, catching fire, dispersing smoke.

Stone, dream, stone

Dreams eat away brain matter when you lay

your head to rest
Is that why those dreams always smelled stale?
Or why lips and eyes that speak of dreams
always smell like a sun-scorched mud field
Dreams that tumble over when pushed

The kind of dream where it doesn't matter
if someone says, that won't make you any
money
Your so-called dream will never come true

A dream that's meaningful because it's pointless
That's the Stone Pillow Principle

Who would sleep on something rock-hard?
We have soft materials lay our heads. Plush
fabrics that sink to the touch
Of course I know this. I know sensible pillows
exist
Cost-effective ones, can-be-ordered-next-day-
shipping ones, made-with-feathers-plucked-
from-ducks-or-geese ones

But my dream requires a stone pillow. A can-be-
lethal-in-one-blow pillow, can-be-turned-to-
a-weapon pillow, knock-you-senseless-with-
a-thud pillow
Pillow dream. A dream of something greater.

Pillow-smothering-pillow dream. Strangled-
then-came-back-to-life dream

Then finally, dream overcomes dream.
Becoming lighter. Sucking life from my
bones, veins, body
I am hollow

A pillow jam-packed with vitality, stained with
blood and excrement
This is my dream

You know pillow-fights as a childish game,
where every hit lands with a giggle

My pillow fight is war. Every hit sends someone
to the grave
Let's talk it out, let's keep the peace, they say
while sliding over paperwork
I slide over a stone pillow in response

This is my language. Back-turned silence.
Dreams, stone, dreams. My language is
redundancy—what's that supposed to mean?
Words shrouded by words
Which walls are you trying to break through?
Is there something else you'd like to shroud
yourself with?

This pillow is made from gallstones. Horse
hooves and bull horns. Yes, that kind of
pillow. Here, touch it. Does it droop? Is it
hard as a rock?
The stone pillow principle
Rolling, tumbling down. Then suddenly, it
halts—a dream that plummets

The Precarious Future of a Yorkshire Terrier

Dogs do not think of the future
When summer arrives
Tongues extended, they're one with the season

When I look at the banner that says,
Save Seoul Innovation Park
I take a moment to perform CPR

Three,
Two,
One, deep breath

There are creatures walking in the park like me
Tongues out

Not offering their opinions

When sun beams pour
Into the downy fur of an old dog in a stroller

The dog isn't thinking about the future
Instead, it hurdles toward the future, faster than
anyone

August
Strings of clouds become a leash
Around the sky, pulled along by the season

I cannot remain as me forever,

And you will be freed from yourself one day too

Stroller wheels squeak
Water sloshes between trees and leaves
Adrift
A dog, lost

By the time this park is replaced by a fifty-story
high-rise building
There will be no Yorkshire Terriers

What does the world have planned for those
little dogs?

Braided gray fur

Squeaky baby carriage wheels

Woof

The dog

Barks for a while

The sound clinging stubbornly somewhere

The Yorkshire Terrier

Runs off with a dead cicada in its mouth

Sun beams

Sun beam

Frightening sun beams

The Old Materialist and the Hospital's One Cucumber Plant

Not too long from now
Hospitals in Korea
Will shut their doors for good

Not because people won't be sick anymore
Because there won't be people anymore

Today
The emergency room is busy as ever
Beyond the window of a Starbucks near Ulsan
  University Hospital

A steady stream of ambulances
Flow into collarbones

Sirens steeped with coffee's stubborn scent

A balding man emerging from an ambulance
Shouting at a firefighter
I'm fine, I said I'm fine!

Across from the man's wincing face
The firefighter does not look at ease
Or heave a sigh of relief

Blaring red lights
Sporadic brake screeches
The act of rescue
A fruit precious until harvested

I like hospitals
And if I escape the long underground tunnel
In front of the Jamsil Bridge

Seoul Asan Hospital appears

To think, there are as many sick people here
As shoppers in Jamsil department store
Or picnickers in Han Gang Park

At the bedside of a great-grandfather awakening
   from cardiac arrest
His family member

Does not rejoice

Su-Young once said
That if the world didn't need poems anymore
That itself would be poetry

I write poems
I can still write more

Prodded along by some stray wind
Before I knew it
I'd arrived at the firefighter's mood

Poetry

Is a balding old man's incessant yelling

This place will not be the last
It's in the middle
The edges, to be precise

Because singing from the corner
Is the inner flesh of a cucumber, pale as ever

With Faith That We've Already Reached Each Other

Well, did you get what you came there for?
They say that person had departed
From the end of an alley of a coastal road

Or maybe some kind of pier
A figure hovered over an empty chair
Dust settling over a chair that lost its home

He looked on for a very long time

And as he looked on,
I, too,
Looked at him for a very long time

So, did you take them in?

Waves slowly departed from shallow waters
Shadows departed

When finally, the smelly dead fish departed

Sunshine's slanted blue lines formed
Along veins of the Sugi tree leaves

Refugees of light traversing outer space in an
  instant

Well, did you end up taking them in?

Moving from one boring airport to another
One life here, another one there
From human, as a human

So, are they adjusting well?

When rounds of applause
Depart from the hands that birthed them

Will it be palms
Or applause
Who do the longing?

Even departed water droplets

End up somewhere on the coast, surely

I'll be writing a letter addressed to sea fog

With faith that we will meet again

With faith that we've already reached each other

Shadows walk the white sand beach
Footprints adjoined to sand

Sound and sound
Arms around shoulders

When firecrackers ignite
And crackling noises grow distant from paper
shells

Some deep darkness of night
Will find those crackling noises
And embrace them

To a Baker

Like wheat bread made by gentle hands
Like a whiff of something baking in the oven

Like the flat, soft shape of a doughy someone

People who loved and
The people they loved
Faced each other in a line

Two clouds of loving flour
Their two curtain skirts
Flapped strongly, but did not stretch

The two lovers thought it a relief

And a pity

Because maybe, love is where relief and pity overlap

Like handprints in dough
Sorrow lingered for a while

Like pale, warm, fluffy affection
Like golden rain clouds

The two clouds looked on as the handprints departed

Radiant,

Beautiful,

Hearts sounding like tambourines

Dry flour's scent swirled over their windowsill

I wanted to tell them, there are people who love
both of you

They are being born again and again

And sorrow is a forgotten plastic chair by a
wheat field

Like golden rain clouds
Like pink curtain shadows shielding their eyes
  from sun

Lazy, bored affection

Congratulations,
Today your cheeks smell like fresh bread

And now
I might tear myself a piece

Spool of Love

What should I do?
I can hear the Earth spinning

My two helixes pick up on a colossal palace's
rotation

A spool of love dispensing dark strings to no
end

The Earth ceaselessly
Turning its massive body

Just as primates in captivity
Pluck out hair after hair

These stars hold no beliefs
This sphere no grand faith

But you say this palace is spinning?
This grand civilization of love?

In reality, love despises love
But the Earth has no self-hatred

Nothing to like and
Nothing to dislike either

What's with this Earth anyway?

No boldness, no plan—what's that about?

When I think of this mess, I can hear grinding
saw teeth
Like the noise of a rotating palace closing in at
three thousand miles an hour

The sound of one single speck of love
Finer than flour, being crushed and smothered

Maybe it's a relief
To be nothing at all

Not to have a predestined discovery of the

universe
Or a need to experience a great love's
tumultuous fall

Autumn showers subside
Water rushes into a stream, releasing an odor

Seen at a distance, this stream is yarn stretching
towards the Earth
Winding into a ball, almost certainly
Spinning endlessly, never resting

When the last torrential rainstorm consumes all
in its path

The Sekai of someday
Will swell and rise with the downpour

The great conveyer belt

But for now, it's just Yuseong Stream
Drying up under scorching sunlight
Swelling with each wet season

Assuming this position

Peaceful Reign of Alpacas

And it came to be that all tragedy was banned
in the Alpaca Kingdom
So was the alpaca king's solemn decree one
afternoon, as white fur floated along the castle
walls
But in the wake of tragedy's persecution, joy
was the first to disappear, like the smell of
coffee escaping with the night. After all, there
was no elation without despair. But that was
precisely the Alpaca King's clever agenda—he
had not intended to eliminate sorrow, but joy.

Just as one drop of oil in the sewers could halt
the city's sadness

Every heart in that country slowly withered away

Traversing the castle's roads was only silence

Looked upon from afar, the town was becoming a sort of jelly. Clear, gelatinous sadness made from sunken sediment in water. A bowl of jelly. And just when the full moon, wearing a necklace of white fur, was about to take a spoonful, sad and gleeful alpacas alike were slaughtered one by one.

Long necks piled in gooey, melty lumps

The alpaca king was satisfied

Now, the citizens will want for nothing. Today shall begin my reign of peace

A country in peaceful reign is cold and unfeeling. It is a place of rigid hand gestures, death, and things that follow. One that's long neglected the living and beating heart of alpacakind. Each passing day went by in prosperity and abundance. The clouds took firm, apathetic shapes. Finally, alpaca citizens made complete what those shapes expressed. They spat silently in the face of factories and families, schools and small alleys. They hacked and spat, then spat again. What they spat out was not death, but life. All kinds of it. Far-reaching droplets of saliva, more permanent than permanence itself.

Part Two:
Into the New World
(A World Re-encountered)

Don’t Have to Speak Nicely

That singer just doesn’t age

As a high school student, I sang along
To verses in “Gee” and “Tell Me”

When I see a beautiful person, I can’t just
compliment anymore
I wonder how much effort that radiant beauty
must have taken

You don’t have to speak nicely

Clock tower, sky crumbling to the tick of a
clock hand, sunset, sky closing in from the

other side, crooked lines, cracks, red and
apricot-colored warmth

The passage by the clock tower, gray stone floors
and wafer crumbs falling on them, flames—
wavering flames

Sweet scents of candy and chewy jjondeugi

Graying hairs sprouting from a teacher's desk,
the scuffles of children's shoes, scattering
sounds, transparent

A certain mood, loaded like a gun

Things both beautiful and terrifying grow
within this school's walls

It's not a good, bad, or beautiful thing
That's just how it is

Yearbooks of every class from first to last, piled
faces squeezed into every picture, changing
color with every touch, naked trees swaying,
unchanging, tepid sunlight flooding in the
backdrop, the lives, the survival, of people

There is a light coming in from outside
Burning everything

Fire, light, allowing everything to grow again

You don't have to speak nicely

Human hearts are as complicated
As they are simple

Pagoda trees, every swaying branch is a painting
when the wind blows

Sometimes, we love because it's the right thing
to do

I walk the school halls by myself sometimes

In grade school, I used to draw schoolhouses
  like rectangles
Simple connections between straight lines

But in the real world,
There are no neat and rectangular schools

Sharp corners jut out suddenly
From back doors and main entrances

For a long time, I wanted to erase
Those far-off, crooked emotions and little
  towns, all of it

But
Now I

Don't have to speak nicely

If the Devil took a giant Monami eraser to those
front and back doors

No one could enter
No one could exit

The smell of scattered crumbs
A school sports field with the lights out

You don't have to speak nicely

Clock towers are not what surrounds you but
A way of taking a walk

Into the New World

1.

Child, I'm trying to fit the whole world into
my eyes. Sounds of eyelids. Rolling pupils.
Straining to fit all the world, all at once, into
two bloodshot eyes

Right now, at this moment, someone is being
born
At this moment, someone is dying

I'm trying to treasure newborn cries and dying
breaths all at once

Some might become the next dictator
Or raise up a flag of liberation
Or wave a lightstick at a concert
Or hold up a dark snake's scale on a night when
a warrant was issued

I realized that to capture the world in my eyes, I
need to be fully immersed
Sounds of pupils dilating. Wavering eyelashes.
My child, my bright night

2.

All things of love

All things of people

Shouldn't all that's sad be beautiful, just like
how all that's beautiful is sad?

Birds fly out
Birds fly in
Heartbeats of migratory birds. Aflame. Heart
and wind in rhythm

3.

Bird Strike
An airplane plummets after collision with birds

Two survivors in the rear end

Coincidence

Destiny

In December, my mind will linger on the
deceased longer than the survivors.

4.

Gyrodrop: Human(s) who find intrigue
in fact that they might just die **Evil**: A
supposition that only garners attention
for being interesting **I Love You Just Like**

This: A permanently ongoing supposition about impossib(ility). **Into the New World**: Lee Myung-bak's acidic shipping container. Hannam Bridge's Kisses. Baek Nam-ki. Martyr. Martyrs. Maybe if I open my eyes, today again…

Efforts to make Good more interesting than Evil.

5.

My child, when the happiness is too much I start to cry, and when the sadness is too much

I start to laugh. I'm walking towards you down
a hallway at the border of comedy and tragedy

Like the empty skeleton of someone who is
thinking
Today the room is empty

I hope you'll come back and fall asleep

With eyes closed, there is nothing inside.
There is something in my eyes so I'm not
looking at what's in front of me. This world
only begins once you open your eyes—yes,
back to the start

May

Child,
Did you know? Flowers bloom because of
shadows

I'm someone who strives to be close to people
near me always saving a spot for someone to
sit always shifts their seat closer to be next to
someone like that

You, child, are the kind of kid who walks over
dirt roads of sadness's flower buds
And the season's blank spaces, seared white
leaves, grass shoots that push spring along
When they see that first mountain magnolia

bloom, roots clinging to the earth.

A flower buries itself at its feet
The botanical struggle, questioning how beauty
becomes nourishment

That isn't to say endings shouldn't be grieved, it's
why they should be all the more
You feel it when a flower stem suddenly loses its
petals

No flower blooms in a place where magnolia
shadows do not live
The flowery light of someone who has overcome

darkness

May
On the sound of footsteps of people gathering
every year

Yes, child, to view May, you should become part
of May—no, you should remind yourself
that you already belong to May's flesh, blood,
petals, and season

Just as the rain-soaked mountain magnolia
carefully counts the raindrops drying on its
body

My child, May, here both dark and bright
belong in the forest of flowering trees. That's
what we'll believe, that is how we'll walk,
that's how we'll go, when sunlight rushes to
the forest's vast side, we will stand beside it
again

And be the ones who stand beside the ones who
comfort

Trick or Treat

Once foul words stick to your body, they don't
fall off so easily

In slumber, when dandelion seeds scatter
A snack truck
falls

The world, even in sadness, demands a right
answer

Incense altar in front of City Hall
There are yesterdays, each with their own faces

Traffic lights spying in hunched positions

Only now do I realize
The idea behind lights

I plan to eat, if it isn't candy
I plan to eat, all of you

One spring evening
Splayed out over the lawn in town square
I thought about the tomorrows of brilliant
  things
Rises and falls
Extravagance
I thought about the yesterdays and futures of

town squares

Candy tends to stick to your teeth
Love tends to stick in your mind

Passing days crumble and turn to dust
At the end of it all
However,

I'll roll out like candy spilled from a box
Like a box's dark interior
Comforting in its secretiveness

Despair does not often side with hope

So try not to be hopeful when taking despair's
hand

I am learning to fall asleep again
The days feel fresh and new

Even if I am walking the same roads as yesterday

Impossible Scraps

So many thread spools tossed aside to knit a
sock

In the sewing factory
Forgotten bodies pile

Loose, swaying ends
That smell
Left aside, piling, cries muffled by layers

Leftover threads spill and unravel
Endlessly

Where have all my scraps gone?

Box hedges
Dirt piles in the yard, vomit
Espresso
Scrapped thoughts

Loves I disdained
Love-hates I took a liking to

None of it matters

I am where I've ended up after sifting and
sifting
Ready-made life

One brilliant afternoon
As the sun sheds its excess light

I talk a walk across blinding rays

What is it to grow—
Is it to remain, or to throw away

To live,
Or to die

The pile of wooden sticks by the wall
Is soaking up the sun's loose threads

Swaying its branches

Leaving its smells and odors to bleed

Instead of growing taller

Summer trees save their strength

So on an afternoon of overthinking

I set my thoughts side by side

It was a coincidence that, in a shop in Seochon

I saw socks made from scrap thread*

Hammering sun beams

Dead-center of light

Surely, all my scraps went to heaven

Because God is mending my next life

Was the sock's small hope

*Sockstaz: Recycled Sock Project

Memory's Home

Even trains have homes

Suseo Railyard

Lines of train cars return at dawn
Thousands of eyes asleep in rows

I walk along the nearby wire fence
A distinct metal smell
Emanating from the border between summer
and spring

A time when seasons take corporeal forms

Do hearts have homes too
With rails
Ones that you can ride along as your mind
vacantly wanders

Trains of thoughts chug along

If even bad memories have their own home
From where
Each memory departs one by one
Returning punctually at dawn

I am a person who wonders how lonely it must
be there

When my formative memories
Swish by, turning over the mounds of my mind

I wonder how that home holds so fast to its
pillars

If its residents were evicted

Front door unlatched
Windows swung open

A voice said, "You, out!"

And just like that, they were gone

I would be the one outside
Who slowly raises a hammer

Who faces the home that abandoned him
And starts striking away

Finally, the house collapses
And when so many livelihoods spill out into the
world

The night sky,
That gaping hole above everyone's heads

Will show everyone:

"Home is here.
Home is there.
That place far away is home.
The vast sky, all the earth and stars, is all our home."

I would then reply:

"I am the only home I have."

Pounding my chest, standing tall and firm

Rail yard

The wind drags its old bones over vast plains

Whirlwinds tear their own limbs along chain-
link fences
Sounds of metal riddled with holes
Graze my ear

And I say once again

"I am my own base.
I am my own storage closet."

Even a home needs a home

Then finally, I can be someone
Who takes their home in

Ghost of Certainty

I don't feel certain about myself today, you tell
me
Certain? But you are fog. Not a silk curtain, not
a Ginko tree. You're breaths of air scattered in
every which way. You are smoke

You, however, are always pulling out your hair.
You are uncertain, cannot trust anything.
Like Trust is the name of a remote hamlet

I asked a question in response
If you do not have certainty, what do you
have in its place? Your legs only tremble in
response. Dead skin flakes fall to the floor

Vagueness more abundant with absence.
Summer's hazy veil. Humidity in July. Water fleas. Roaring black flames
Inauspicious black hairs embroidered with fog

Would it be right for a broom to wish it was a dustpan?
Or for a tart to wish it was a cube of *kkakdugi*?
Or for a coffee bean to envy a pea? Well, would it? So…
But you shake your head again. No. I said, no. Nevermind. You swing your hair like a propellor
Sending a white shroud into mid-air like a

helicopter.
Saying those aren't the kind of questions that
have to do with certainty
You say you don't know what to do
I tried to approach you slowly. Like an alligator
lurking in a tea-steeped bath. Like a teaspoon
smoothing out ripples in water
I saw the floor become a river. Touched a
musical scale made of leaves. Even in
moments when I was uncertain what to do
There are things that will happen no matter
what, right?
Trust is another name for a dark, spiny
pufferfish. Scraping by somewhere in our

ocean depths. But you keep saying no. No,
no, no!
Like you're growing a tree made of negation.
Like someone fighting your way through a
thick jungle. You keep saying "no"
The nametag was slowly transforming into the
word "no"

The two letters of n-o are being frantically sewed
onto your forehead and mine

So I just said, yes it is
Without even knowing what it was
Or what it should have been

In an ensemble of yes's and no's
Our lips scattered apart. So far away that no one
could say who was right and who wasn't.
From two identical necks

Yes it is
No it isn't
I said, it isn't. I said, it *is*
Transforming into Adam's apples, the only thing
that was for certain

Future of the End

The lamp a gorgeous hue
Two legs pale as a sheet

Pale, thin scissor blades crossing
Dangling and slicing the sun's microscopic dust

Morning and misfortune, a strangely well-suited
word pair

I can't believe that you disappeared
Or that one day news of your disappearance will
disappear
And my memory of that news will disappear
with me

And that the daytime moon
Which slowly watched our disappearance
Will disappear into blurry blankness

Death is a definite substance
That reeks of metal

To forget what one hated
Is to lose what one loved

In your room, lightning struck daily like
 migraines
Faint figures moving with scallop-soft skin
Voices

Tones that slipped out on occasion

What to do about the smell of skin lingering
  where someone once was?
To where do hunched imprints on floors
And yellowing people-patterns move on?

Let's not forgive bad people any more
But to consider this
I have to trust the worst person within me

Pale legs multiplied to hundreds
Thousands
Tens of thousands

Clicking sounds form a river, the rising sun
crosses

The future of the end

Roots of green raddish sprouts
Slowly inching their way into darkness

Cocoa Afterlife

Cocoa powder landed on my forehead
So I came back to life

I still do not know which ovule is right for my
soul

This morning, I can imagine how Buddha or
Jesus felt
But I still love us even more than God

If I could disappear again
I'd like to be a young ray of sun on a cacao
plant

If I must be born again
I'd like to be a speck of light brown on a cacao
   seed

There are so many people everywhere I go
Far too many people

I cannot believe that the world is not heaven
But to think that it isn't even hell—

I am always asking how that cocoa powder
   granule is doing

Not the smell of people, not their heartbeats,

not their movements and rhythms,
Not their peaceful silences and pale colors, none
of it

Cocoa is ground powder made from Cacao
beans
I'm constantly being born again
As a human, I keep waking up in human form

Chocolate cake is sweeter with a pinch of salt
Pain goes great with the word Happiness

So it's not a coincidence that shadows and
chocolate share similar hues?

I open my eyes here in the cocoa afterlife

To Newborn Demons

More good demons than bad roam this world
Unfortunately,
I mumble again, and again
In front of the blackboard

But truth be told, I've come across some terrible
demons
Washing rice
Feeding and clothing their children
Getting fouler by the minute
Without casting even a shadow

But faith
Is not the sum of what has been, but what will

be

Standing before the pitch-black chalkboard
I've been sucked into that dark expanse before
but

To open the door
You need the resolve to open it
Before the door opens
It has to make a sound
And so
The blackboard is a door
A thing that can be opened or closed

Which is right,
To say the truth
Or to say what needs to be true?

Footprints left by newborn born demons
When you take a magnet to them
They'll be lifted
Above chalk dust

They make unruly noises

Many hesitant steps once existed
Between left foot and right

If you knock quietly on my heart
There are places where it opens gently in a
continuous line

There are countless swaying red ears of rice
And before you know it

Like snow piled secretly in a corner
Sometimes
You are lying face-down

In some classroom of neither hope nor
disappointment
Crouching low

Are little demons pouring out their hearts'
  sounds

One sweep of a broom suddenly
Stirs up a blood-red blizzard beyond the window

That
Is the power of our hesitation
The flavor of rice ears turned to ash

Somewhere between rain and snow, cemeteries
  and burial mounds, litterers and trash
  collectors, growing and withering trees, you
  and me, strangers and humidity,

I wanted to teach

Walk

If nothing else, your anguish belongs to you
That is your rage
Your heartbreak, your grief, your pain

Sometimes
Clouds become big white magnets
And draw in light

That's the work of demons, not angels
It's Anguish who rose to the occasion

So don't forget:
In the universe, there is much more darkness
    than light

Ears of rice let out foul odors as they ripen
Because they know of good things

To be what "dead tree" means in flower language
To press a singed candlewick to your tongue,
Become a candle, and burn

POET'S NOTE

1.

One of Butler's most prominent propositions could be found in her discovery that a thesis is only made possible by antithesis. There can be no hope without despair, no darkness without the presence of light. I have often recalled despair in hopes of being reminded of love.

That was natural.

And it's thoughts like these that have, at times, comforted me.

3.

Snow flurried into the early hours of dawn, when a sliver of light entered the window. Tapping away at a crack in the darkness. Finally breaking through. Reaching far into a place that contained only pitch-black. Where had the light come from, when nearly nothing could be seen outside?

I wondered—could this have meant that someone, somewhere had discovered light even on the darknest of nights? Or was it a sign that no matter how dark the night was, a stubborn light would always remain? But upon closer inspection, I found the light had not come from outside at all.

What I saw was the reflected light of my entryway glinting in the window as I rose out of bed. A façade originating from inside.

It was hope, borne of my own movement.

Only then did I stop looking outside and begin to look inward. Hope from the inside. Aflame. Frightening. Flaming tongues brought to existence by motion.

2.

Cheerfulness: Resistance of a situation in which optimism is impossible.

Cuteness: Cuteness to the point of stubbornness, a kind of battle.

Sweetness: The deadliest weapon in my arsenal.

Poems: All of these are written by you.

POET'S ESSAY

1.

A dog on a walk often looks back at its owner. As though the owner's face were his own. Almost as thought to confirm its own existence.

A lakeside park. A gentle breeze carries the smell of water. Flocking birds. Sounds of feet walking leisurely along a path.

They say that dogs don't recognize themselves in the mirror. Some claim this is proof dogs have no ego. But what if the dog considers its ego to be the other, and not the self? I couldn't help but think this when I saw the dog look back at its owner. I considered a world in which one existed only as the "other." For a soul's existence to hinge on the presence of another. I pondered a consciousness founded upon complete, utter trust and close bonds with another being.

And then:

Woof.

With a bark, the dog lunged forward.

Ripping apart my mind's curtain.

2.

But sometimes, we love because it is the right thing to do.

Some states of being are possible only because you do not know me, and I do not know you. Like strangers on our daily commutes, we rub shoulders but can only guess what each other's lives are like.

The subway car rattles.

There are communities that are completed by the fact its members do not bother to approach or accost one other. And in this world, there are moments that can be explained only by vagueness, obscurity, and events we do not know nor try to know. That is, if we can even call that an explanation at all.

I am considering this when the iron bridge over Han River comes into view.

Another chance moment, a gap made possible by hesitation. Two bridges stacked together, separated by a thin space. Wind, light, darkness, sound, waves and souls pass through.

A cramped, narrow space.

Who could be living in there?

I'm certain a poem must live, at least, in that momentary curiosity.

3.

What does it mean to write…?

I write because… there are wishes that have never come true, certain things that never materialized.

This is not aestheticism, or even art for art's sake.

…It is sympathy towards life.

4.

There is no special power to poetry.

It is much more difficult to admit the absence of poetry's power than to believe in it blindly.

Only when I choose to accept this does poetry start to possess a certain power.

COMMENTARY

Constructed Futures

Song Hyun-ji (Literary Critic)

Hello, Byeon Yun-je. It's nice to finally meet you.

Often in the afterword of a poem collection, a person of close relation to the poet broadens the scope of the work by contextualizing it within the author's life and providing readers with a closer look into the text. When I was asked to write the afterword of your second poem collection, "Anti-Nationalists," I had to think for a long time about what I would write. You and I have never met, and aside from the private, one-sided kinship I developed towards you while reading your first collection, *I Plan on Being Just as Lovely Next Year*, we share no personal ties. But then I remembered a definition of poem as a place that encompasses the innermost recesses of a poet's mind. I regained courage from the thought that if I wanted to dive deeper into the mind of Byeon Yun-je the poet, the shortest path to doing so would be to read his poems. I'll begin this afterword by recalling the day I encountered your first poem collection.

You titled your first collection *I Plan on Being Just as Lovely Next Year.* I confess that this title initially puzzled me, in that the word "plan" implies a sense of certainty about the future while the phrase "just as lovely" similarly seems to reflect a strange self-assuredness in its assessment of the present. I was at first bewildered, and then envious that someone could make such a resolute statement about the present and future. I wondered: if Byeon Yun-je and I lived in the same universe, why did Schrodinger's cat seem to exist for him and not for me? Tortured by the thought that I was the problem, I wanted to know the reason why we had arrived at such different conclusions and discover what could make such an affirmative statement possible. The only way I could do so was to read your poem collection, which undoubtably contained many of your privately held thoughts and considerations. To me, your title seemed to convey something about your past, present and future at the same time.

It wasn't long until I concluded that the title did not actually convey certainty but belief—or rather, an active effort to believe. For instance, in "Out-Boxer: Ms. Alpaca's Reply," Byun presents a universe in which there is no safety, no realness, no love, not even "proof that a cat was ever there." How could someone have certainty while being aware that nothing in this world can be certain and that everything is an illusion? Once my thoughts had progressed this far, I felt a bit closer to you as a person. After all, deep despair and extreme optimism are like two sides of one coin. It hit me that under all of that self-assured language was a desperate effort to come out of your situation with a sense of optimism.

But upon reading your more recent works, I wonder if even those efforts have reached their limits. In your most recent collection, you seem to reflect more prominently on the dismal present and as a response, express an even more adamant resolve. In your previous collection's closing poem, "The Stay-Still Club that Can't Stay Still," you draw attention to the violence imbued in the words "stay still," pointing out that the "stay-still club" cannot stay "still" any longer. But in your recent works, you seem to speak even more strongly about what can be made possible by action. I am sure many recent events and social issues have led to this shift, among them the 12.3 insurrection (Anti)Nationalist, redevelopment of Seoul Innovation Park ("The Precarious Future of Yorkshire Terriers"), low-birth rate crisis ("The Old Materialist and the Hospital's One Cucumber Plant"), a rapidly worsening climate crisis ("Precious, Island; "Spool of Love"), and unjust termination and employment scams ("Sinister Soy Sauce Poem"). But in contextualizing your work within a broader social context, you display a will to move closer to a place of optimism rather than simply recite a list of social issues.

Perhaps that's why I thought of the poet Kim Su-Young while reading this collection. You quote one of Kim Su-Young's poems in "The Old Materialist and the Hospital's One Cucumber Plant" but I also thought of his poem "Snow" (I read a few of Byun's poems alongside Kim Su-Young's poems—for one, I read "The Future and Anxiety of Yorkshire Terriers," which described "frightening sun beams," alongside Kim Su-Young's verse, "a hot day / is like a sea sponge called enemy." Maybe the similarity can be found in your abilities to embody both satirical and subversive qualities. As I am sure you know, Kim wrote three different poems called "Snow." The "Snow" that comes to my mind now is the most recently written of the three.

Snow falls and falls again

After some thought, there it falls again

Will snow fall after I cry like a baby?

After so much thought, there it falls again

Will snow fall after one line, then the next?

Will snow fall over ruin after ruin?

(Hanguk Munhak, 1966 Summer Edition)

The poem's speaker looks on as snow falls before him, and expresses doubt over whether the snow will continue. And so he asks: "will snow fall after I cry like a baby?" There seems to be a time jump after he raises this initial question, after which he confirms that the snow did indeed fall ("After so much thought, there it falls again"). But of course, this single observation does not put an end to his doubts. The poem ends with the question, "will snow fall over ruin after ruin?" In summary, the speaker confirms reality over the first two stanzas, voices suspicion in the third, confirms reality again in fourth, then expresses doubt again in the fifth and sixth stanzas The poem's structure seems to suggest that doubt is slowly taking over the speaker's mind. But considering that the poem established a pattern of returning to a confirmed observation of reality, I also think he may have chosen to exclude the moment the speaker confirms that the snow "falls over ruin after ruin." Perhaps Kim Su-Young is waiting for the reader to envision the scene themselves, or it could be that he himself is waiting, with bated breath, to see the snow fall. If in this work, snow falling is likened to the act of writing a poem, I might even venture to say that Kim Su-Young was a poet who wrote poems with the goal of assuring us that snow really would "fall ruin over ruin."

I would like to liken Kim Su-Young's poetic journey to yours in *Anti-Nationalist*. This is because it felt as though this collection is a continuation of the hope-like belief that you presented in your first collection. At a time when attempts to look positively toward the future are being constantly thwarted, you offer a new approach. To discuss any of this, we inevitably have to begin with the complicated subject of quantum mechanics. In "You Don't Have to Speak Nicely," "Into the New World" and "May," you continually speak from a quantum mechanical perspective, viewing the world in terms of superposition, or overlapping states. What's interesting is that you first split the world into binaries. In the first poem alone, you present the world as a place at "the border of comedy and tragedy" by dividing the subjects of the poem into opposing pairs, such as "newborn cries and dying breaths," the " next dictator[s]" and those who "raise up a flag of liberation," things that are "beautiful" and "sad," birds that "fly in" and "fly out," the affairs of the "living" and the "dead," "good" and "evil" and so on. As a result, I begin to view the world as an "ensemble of yes's and no's" (from "Ghost of

Certainty").

Another notable point is your emphasis on the actions of individuals that reside within this world you've designed. Your previous collection highlighted the role of the speaker ("I") as an observer within the world of quantum mechanics, in which a subject's "state becomes fixed" in the "moment that someone looks"(from "Quantum Mechanical, Mermaid") (this was, of course, to criticize the system of labor that deprives workers of the ability to view a subject, thereby eliminating the possibility for new existence). However, this collection seems to center its focus more intently on the agency of the self. It continually turns its attention to the role of the individual ("I") as someone that can "exert influence on the position and movement of another object,"* asking questions such as "what is the difference between seeing and viewing?" (from "Today's Wonder").

Just as Karen Barad, based on Niels Bohr's quantum mechanics, posited relational ontology, I would like to point out how this collection of poems centers on the relational nature of the self. Unlike in the previous collection, in which the indeterminacy of the subject was center focus, in this one the observer ("I") is treated not as a fixed entity but a relational being that is abstract and ever-changing. Lines like "to view May, you should become part of May" (from "May"), or "to capture the world in my eyes, I need to be fully immersed" (from "Into the New World") show that you view

* For more on observers, the act of observing and Karen Barad's theory, see Park, Junyeong, *Neo-materialism: politics and material ontology* (Greenbee, 2023).

the self as a constructed being—"a kind of material arrangement, or a part of such an arrangement."* As constituents of a dynamically (re)forming world, we collaborate in the formation of that world— which means that even if we are alone, we are "alone together" (from "Airbnb").

The last line of "Into the New World" takes on a new meaning when seen under this light: "With eyes closed, there is nothing inside… this world only begins once you open your eyes." While this can be read as a reminder of the importance of facing reality with open eyes, it also points to the fact that the self exists only in relation to the world, and that similarly, the world cannot be described outside of its relationship to oneself.

* Ibid., 404,

To summarize, your most recent poem collection portrays the world as indeterminate, emphasizes the possibilities of individual action driven by a hope for a better world and displays an intense effort to believe in those possibilities. This collection, which denounces a society "that's long neglected the living and beating heart of alpacakind" (from "Peaceful Reign of Alpacas") and reiterates that the act of not "staying still" can significantly change the world, reaffirms that Byeon Yun-je is not a poet who is "hopeful when taking despair's hand" (from "Trick or Treat") or simply looks towards an idealized world with a vague sense of optimism. Rather, he is a poet who dreams of the future through actively living it day by day. The future-tense sentences that fill the poems of this collection do not describe an existing future but the "sum of... what will be" or "what needs to be true" (from "Newborn Demons"). In a time when countless poems are predicting the end, your poems picture the "future of the end." And now I wonder: can this dream that I found while reading your poems become a rock hard enough to withstand the weight of the world? Although I don't know the answer that question, I've started to believe that such a future is possible and want to join you in building this future.

Previously, I mentioned Kim Su-Young's speaker in "Snow," who wondered whether the snow would fall over ruins. I speculated that Kim may have spent his entire life writing poems to make that snowfall possible. Perhaps good poems are all connected somehow, because through reading your poems I understand his poems better, and similarly I read your poems through the lens of his. I recall that the speakers of your poems incite "snowstorms" by shaking "blankets," "white pages" and "blizzards." I have a feeling that it's not only "nationalists" that will be hit by "Massive, microscopic, and yet tremendous white particles" (from "(Anti)Nationalist"). Rather, all people, hit by that snow, will wake up and begin to see our interconnected world with renewed clarity. And through your poems, you have become a flame illuminating the world around you, ensuring that there isn't a single place—not even the ruins—that light cannot touch.

You are constructing the future with poems of snow. And if the new world we are entering is anything like what you describe, I suppose won't have to stay envious for long. Because I, too, will be lovely next year.

PRAISES FOR
BYEON YUN-JE

Byeon Yun-je's first poem collection *I Plan on Being Just as Lovely Next Year* concerns itself with the dissection of the many images and words encompassed by a single scenario or context. As one example, "The Stay-Still Club that Can't Stay Still" presents rewriting as a method of resisting language's authority by means of substitution. This poem in particular stands out among recent works of poetry related to the Sewol Ferry Tragedy. With words at his disposal, Byeon chips away at the authority of those in positions of power. Rather than openly declaring this resistance, he depicts the process of escaping from the conditions implicated in the word "stillness," paving the way for new possibilities of poetic expression.

–Choi sunkyo, "Words Renewed and a Future Re-written"
Changjakgwabipyeong (Spring 2024 Edition)

In Byeon Yun-je's collection of poems *I Plan on Being Just as Lovely Next Year* (Munhakdongnae, 2023), the narrator of "Ordinary Events" assumes the nonchalant attitude of someone who tries to write off their experiences as "ordinary." Similarly to how "Alpaca Community" evokes the idea of community through the imagery of alpacas, idealizing a form of solidarity founded upon diversity and the individual's escape from oppression, Byeon gives the reader a chance to see life in a new light by way of destruction imbued by ordinariness.

–Lee Byung-Kook "non-humanity, the expansion of the visible world appropriated by animals" *Pureunsangsa* (Spring 2024 Edition)

K-POET

Anti-Nationalist

Written by Byeon Yun-je
Translated by Julie Wi
Published by ASIA Publishers
Address 445, Hoedong-gil, Paju-si, Gyeonggi-do, Korea
Email bookasia@hanmail.net
ISBN 979-11-5662-317-5 (set) | 979-11-5662-794-4 (04810)
First published in Korea by ASIA Publishers 2025

*This book is published with the support of the Literature Translation Institute of Korea (LTI Korea).